MAGNIFICENT
MOBILES

CREATE YOUR OWN MOBILE MASTERPIECES IN EASY-TO-MAKE STAGES

MELANIE WILLIAMS

CHARTWELL
BOOKS, INC.

A QUINTET BOOK

Published by Chartwell Books
A Division of Book Sales, Inc.
114 Northfield Avenue
Raritan Center
Edison, N.J. 08818

This edition produced for sale
in the U.S.A., its territories
and dependencies only.

ISBN 0–7858–0151–0

This book was designed and produced by
Quintet Publishing Limited
6 Blundell Street
London N7 9BH

Creative Director: Richard Dewing
Designer: James Lawrence
Project Editor: Helen Denholm
Editor: Ruth Baldwin
Photographers: Paul Forreseter/Laura Wickenden

Typeset in Great Britain by
Central Southern Typesetters, Eastbourne
Manufactured in Singapore by
Bright Arts Pte Ltd
Printed in Singapore by
Star Standard Pte Ltd

CONTENTS

INTRODUCTION

A mobile is a hanging structure that can be made of one object or of several. When it is suspended, it should be able to move freely in the air currents. Although mobiles are often associated with children – indeed they are sometimes hung above babies' cribs – they make beautiful decorations for any room in the house. You can hang them from a hook in the ceiling or underneath a shelf.

The mobile projects featured in this book use diverse techniques and lots of different themes. None of them requires specialized skills, they are great fun to make, and many of them would be ideal for a group of people to work on. Each project gives a list of the materials you will need at the beginning and has clear, step-by-step instructions and pictures for you to follow. Templates are provided wherever they are required. If these are half size, you will need to enlarge them either by measuring them and doubling the dimensions or by enlarging them by 50 percent on a photocopier.

TECHNIQUES AND MATERIALS

A variety of techniques is used in the book in order to create different effects, but they are all relatively simple. Some of the mobiles are made of cardboard and simply require shapes to be cut out, stuck together and decorated. Others employ simple sewing skills. Three-dimensional shapes are achieved by folding cardboard, using yarn to make pompoms, sewing and stuffing shapes, and creating papier-mâché structures. All of these skills are easy to master – even if you have not used them before.

The only important point about the materials you use is that they should not be

BELOW: Here are some of the basic materials you will need: cutting mat, craft knife, different thicknesses of wire, fine-grit sandpaper, pliers, scissors, white craft glue, varnish, paint brushes, paints, palette, pens, adhesive tape, and masking tape.

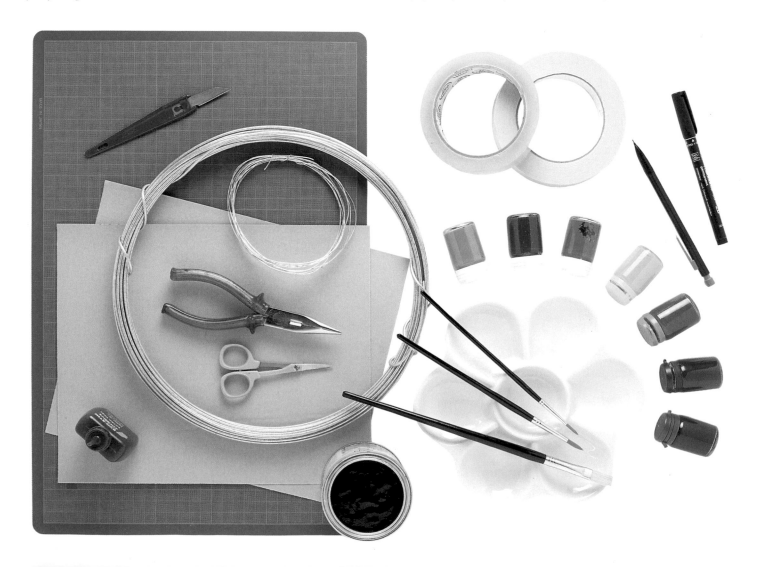

A B O V E : Useful small items for decoration and hanging are glitter, paper clips, screw-in hooks, colored thread, feathers, tissue paper, and a wide selection of beads.

heavy. The lighter they are, the more easily your mobile will move – even in the slightest breeze. Paper, cardboard, tissue paper, fabric, balsa wood, foil, papier-mâché, and wire are all suitable for making the structure of a mobile. There are any number of materials that you can use for decoration. Remember that it will often be suspended from a ceiling or a shelf, so items that reflect light – like sequins or glitter paint – will make it stand out and catch the eye.

HANGING YOUR MOBILE

Hanging a mobile is the most exciting stage in the construction process. This is the moment when your mobile metamorphoses from a static pile of objects and threads to a moving, suspended creation. In the projects that follow, a number of ways of hanging a mobile are shown – all of them easy to make. There is the simple circular "wheel" made of wire from which objects are hung. Cardboard cones and squares are used, too, as well as the more traditional structures which are based on a series of hanging struts.

Achieving a well-balanced mobile is really very simple. When you first hang it up, it may seem a bit lopsided, but this is easily rectified by slightly changing the position of the hanging elements. If a mobile is hanging too much to one side, then you simply need to move more of the weight to the other to adjust the balance. You can also change the length at which the objects are hanging; the only important thing to remember is that they should not bump each other as they move.

The projects in this book will hopefully provide you with inspiration to go on to make your very own mobiles. You can add your own ideas to them and experiment with different sizes and hanging arrangements. Use the techniques as a basis for your own projects and mobilize your imagination!

HAPPY BIRTHDAY

While decorating for a birthday party with balloons and streamers, why not include this simple-to-make, cake mobile? Crumpled tissue paper, paints, and posterboard are all you need. For a personal touch, you could paint a name or message on the cake.

1 Trace the three templates for the cake tiers from this book, enlarge them to full size, and cut them out. Use them as guides to draw the shapes on a sheet of posterboard. Cut out the shapes.

2 Spatter both sides of the three cake-tier shapes with colored poster paint – we used yellow and pink. To do this, hold the brush of watery paint about 1 inch away, bend back the bristles with your fingertip, then let them spring back.

3 Paint a design of your choice on all six sides of the cake tiers. You can draw pencil guidelines first if you like.

4 Cut the tissue paper into 4 × 5 inch squares and crumple them into little balls. Glue the balls, alternating the colors, to the top and bottom edge of the sides of the cake tiers.

TEMPLATES HALF SIZE

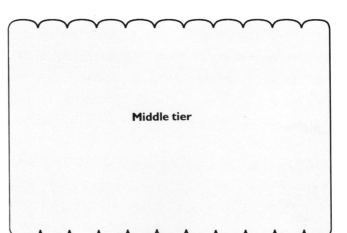

Bottom tier

Middle tier

Candle

5 Make twelve small bows from the narrow ribbon and attach two to each side of each tier.

6 Trace the candle template from the book, enlarge it, and transfer it to a piece of white cardboard. Cut out the candle shape, then paint it.

7 Thread a needle, tie a knot in the end of the thread, and sew twice through the top of the bottom tier (the biggest). Then sew through the bottom of the second tier, twice again for extra security, and knot the thread. Attach the top tier to the middle tier in the same way.

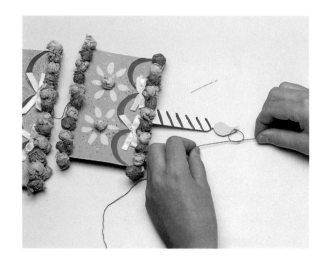

8 Glue the candle to the middle of the top tier, concealing its base behind the tissue-paper balls. Allow the glue to dry thoroughly. Using a needle and thread, sew through the candle flame and tie a knot to secure the thread. The mobile will hang from this.

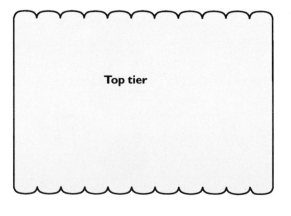

Top tier

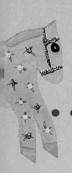

CAROUSEL

Recreate the cheerful atmosphere of the fairground by using brightly colored poster paints, sequins, beads, and glitter pens to decorate this merry-go-round. The five prancing horses are suspended from a simple cardboard cone.

● YOU WILL NEED

- Pair of compasses
- Pencil
- 11 × 16 inch piece of white posterboard
- Scissors
- White craft glue
- Masking tape
- Poster paints
- Mixing palette
- Paint brushes in several sizes
- Glitter pens
- Sequins
- Tracing paper
- 11 × 16 inch piece of white mat board
- Craft knife and cutting mat
- Long-nosed pliers
- 5 feet of thin wire with a metallic finish in two or three different colors
- About 12 colored beads
- Needle

1 Using a pair of compasses set at 6 inches, draw a circle with a diameter of 12 inches on the white posterboard and cut it out.

2 Cut a wedge out of the circle of posterboard. It should look like a slice of cake and be about one-sixteenth of the circle. Draw a wavy line around the edge of the circle and cut along this line.

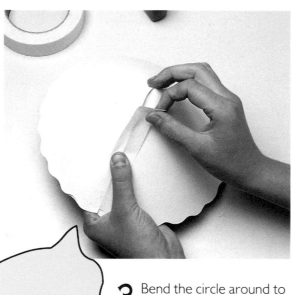

3 Bend the circle around to make a cone shape for the top of the carousel. Place a line of glue along the straight edge where you removed the wedge and lap the other straight edge over it. Press firmly and hold in place with a strip of masking tape until the glue dries. You will need to trim the wavy line where the edges of the board have overlapped.

4 Use a pencil to mark lightly on the cone the guidelines of your chosen design. Paint in blocks or strips of color.

Horse

TEMPLATE FULL SIZE

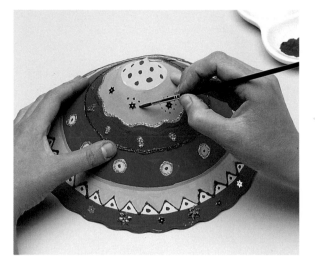

5 Use glitter pens to add more decoration and to emphasize the divisions between colors.

6 Once you have completed the cone, glue sequins around the edge. You may also like to add dots of paint to complete the effect. Paint the inside of the cone with a color that matches one used on the outside.

7 Trace the horse template from this book and cut it out. Use it as a guide to draw five horses on a piece of white mat board. Cut these out using a craft knife and cutting mat.

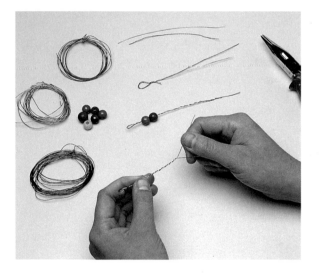

8 On both sides of each horse, lightly pencil in the hooves, mane, tail, and saddle. Now paint the main body of each horse in your chosen color.

9 Paint in the mane, hooves, tail, and saddle, again on both sides. Paint more detail on the body and add the bridle. Use the glitter pens and sequins to add the finishing touches. Allow to dry.

10 To make each pole from which the horses hang, use pliers or scissors to cut two pieces of colored wire about 5½ inches and 5 inches long, one ½ inch longer than the other (this will be used to create a loop at the top). Twist the wires together, making a loop at the bottom. Thread a couple of beads onto the twisted wires for decoration. Repeat until you have six poles; one of these will be used to hang the carousel.

11 Make six little loops from colored wire, using pliers or scissors to cut it. Use a large needle to make two holes in the top edge of each horse's back. Take one of the wire loops you have just made and hook it over the looped end of one of the twisted wire poles. Add a dab of glue to each end of the wire loops and insert them into the two holes you have just made in the horse's back. Repeat this for every horse (the sixth loop is for hanging the carousel). Allow to dry.

12 Use a needle to make five holes at regular intervals around the edge of the carousel. To attach the horses, simply push the ends of the twisted wire poles through the holes you have just made in the carousel and twist them around until they are secure. Place the last wire loop and twisted wire pole into the top of the carousel, using glue to secure the loop as in step 11. Allow to dry. Bend the top of the twisted wire pole into a loop so that the carousel can be suspended.

BUSY BEES

Fluffy pompoms successfully conjour up the texture and character of busy bees. Suspend them around a hive made of paper and twine for an amusing and eye-catching mobile.

● YOU WILL NEED

- Tracing paper
- Pencil
- 8 × 10 inch piece of thin cardboard, as from a cereal box
- Scissors
- Yellow and black yarn, a large ball of each color
- Black felt-tip pen
- 8 × 10 inch piece of white paper
- White craft glue
- Newspaper
- Masking tape
- Ball of twine
- Yellow and black poster paints
- Mixing palette
- Paint brushes in several sizes
- 2 feet galvanized wire, 1/16 inch in diameter
- Silver spray paint
- 2 feet galvanized wire, 1/25 inch in diameter
- Long-nosed pliers
- Yellow sewing thread

1 Trace the pompom template from this book and cut it out. Use this to draw twelve circles on thin cardboard and cut them out.

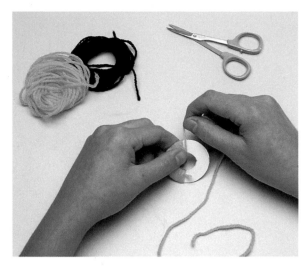

2 To make each pompom, put two of the circles together and wind layers of yarn around them as follows: a single layer of yellow, a double layer of black, and then a final single layer of yellow.

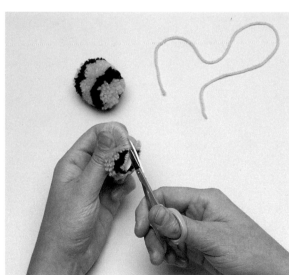

3 When you have finished winding the yarn, use sharp scissors to cut around each pompom through the layers of yarn and between the two circles of cardboard.

4 Tie each pompom tightly with a length of yarn placed between the two pieces of cardboard, making a double knot. Now carefully cut into the cardboard circles to remove them from the pompoms. You may need to trim away loose bits of yarn.

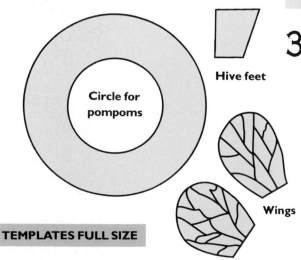

Circle for pompoms

Hive feet

Wings

TEMPLATES FULL SIZE

5 Use the wing template in this book to copy six pairs of wings on tracing paper, then draw the pattern on each wing with a black felt-tip pen. Also draw six pairs of eyes using the black pen on white paper. Cut out all of these. Attach the wings and eyes to the pompom bodies using a small amount of glue.

6 To make the beehive, crumple a large sheet of newspaper into a cone or beehive shape. Bind it with masking tape to help it keep its shape.

7 Place the paper cone on a piece of thin cardboard and draw around the bottom. Cut out this circle.

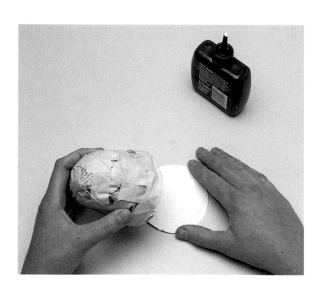

8 Glue the cardboard circle firmly to the base of the cone. Then cover the whole cone shape except the base with glue.

9 Begin to wind twine carefully around the whole of the cone shape, starting at the bottom. When you reach the top, add a little more glue, cut off the end of the twine and tuck it under neatly.

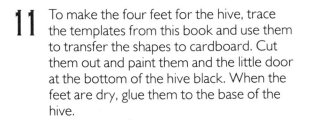

10 When the glue has dried, paint the whole hive, including the base, with yellow poster paint.

11 To make the four feet for the hive, trace the templates from this book and use them to transfer the shapes to cardboard. Cut them out and paint them and the little door at the bottom of the hive black. When the feet are dry, glue them to the base of the hive.

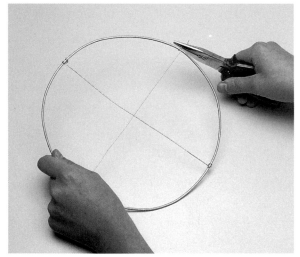

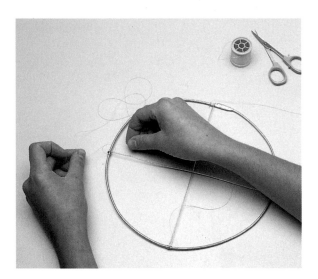

12 From the thicker wire, make a circle about 7½ inches in diameter. Join the ends with masking tape and spray or paint it with silver paint to match the wire.

13 Cut two pieces of thinner wire about 8½ inches long and use them to form a cross across the circle. Attach the cross by bending the wire around the edge of the circle using long-nosed pliers.

14 Tie four pieces of yellow thread to each of the places where the thinner wires are joined to the circle. Knot them at the top so that the wire frame hangs level.

15 Cut a length of thread for each bee, thread it with a needle, knot the end, then pull the needle through the center of the bee's body. The bee will hang from this.

16 Attach a length of thread to the top of the beehive by passing a threaded needle twice through it and securing with a knot. Attach this thread to the center of the wire frame. Then tie the bees at regular intervals but at different heights around the wire frame.

MIRÓ MASTER-PIECE

Bring out the artist in yourself by using works of art as a source of inspiration. This minimalist mobile was inspired by the abstract images of the painter Joan Miró. Colored paper shapes and black rods work well in conveying the deceptively simple lines of modern art.

● YOU WILL NEED

- Tracing paper
- Pencil
- 8 x 10 inch pieces of posterboard in the following colors: yellow, red, black, blue
- Scissors
- 3 wooden skewers
- Black poster paint
- Mixing palette
- Paint brush
- White craft glue
- Needle
- Strong black button thread

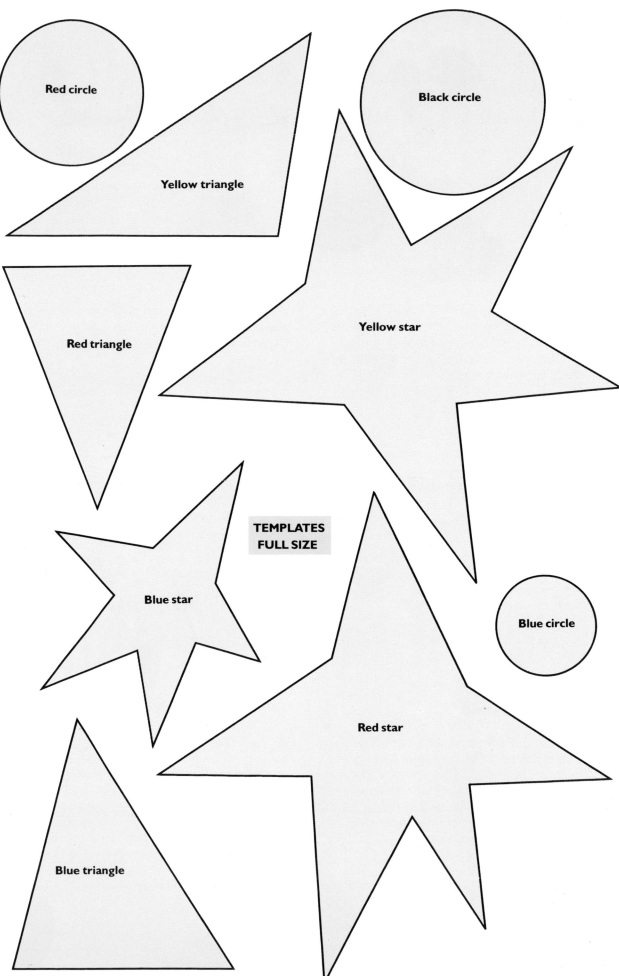

Red circle

Black circle

Yellow triangle

Red triangle

Yellow star

Blue star

TEMPLATES FULL SIZE

Blue circle

Red star

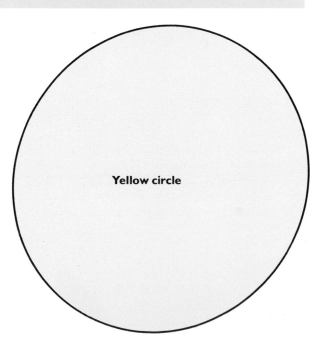

Yellow circle

Blue triangle

1 Trace the templates of the shapes from this book and cut them out. Place the templates on the correct color posterboard (the color is noted on each template) and cut out two of each shape using scissors.

2 Cut the pointed ends off the wooden skewers using sharp scissors. Now paint them with black poster paint; they will form the struts.

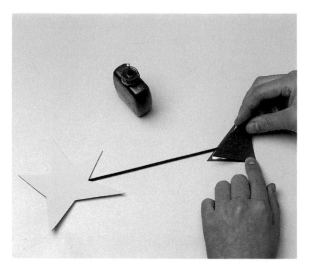

3 To create the top strut, spread glue over the surface of one yellow star and stick it to the end of one of the black sticks, then glue the other yellow star over the first one so that the stick comes from the middle of the finished star. Repeat this process with the blue triangles at the other end of the stick.

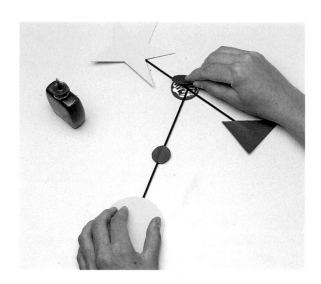

4 Following the method outlined in step 3, attach the big yellow and small blue circles to another black stick in the positions shown: this will form the downward strut. Now join the top and downward struts together at a slight angle, covering the meeting point with the two red circles glued together.

5 Glue the two blue star pieces together and repeat for the red triangle pieces. Attach them to the shapes on the top strut, using a needle threaded with strong black button thread with a knot in the end. Push the needle twice through the blue star and triangle and then through the edge of the shapes at each end of the strut. Unthread the needle and tie the thread in a secure double knot. Trim off any excess thread.

6 To form the unattached strut, follow the method outlined in step 3 to glue the red star, yellow triangle, and black circle to the remaining black stick at slightly different angles, so that when the stick is laid down it will not lie flat. Secure a thread through the top of the black circle, using the needle to guide the thread through, and fasten it with a double knot.

7 Attach the strut made in step 6 to one of the points of the yellow star, using a needle as before. Attach a long piece of thread to the top of the red circle in the same way; the mobile will hang from this. The point on the red circle at which you attach the hanging thread will affect the angle at which the mobile hangs.

THE GALAXY

What could be a more suitable theme for a mobile than a representation of our galaxy? Foil-covered stars, a papier-mâché-covered balloon and a painted ping-pong ball have been used here to depict the planets and stars. For this project you can improvise with the shapes of the stars and the zigzag.

● YOU WILL NEED

- Balloon
- Flour and water
- Bowl
- Newspaper
- Dressmaker's pin
- Fine-grit sandpaper
- White latex paint
- Poster paints of various colors, including gold
- Mixing palette
- Small and medium paint brushes
- Pair of compasses
- Pencil
- Sheet of thin cardboard, any color
- Colored felt-tip pens (optional)
- White craft glue
- Paper clips
- Long-nosed pliers
- 11 x 16 inch piece of white mat board
- 8 x 10 inch piece of gold foil paper
- Scissors
- Craft knife and cutting mat (optional)
- 11 x 16 inch piece of black mat board
- Ping-pong ball
- Silver thread
- Needle

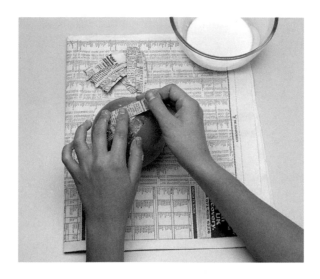

1 Blow up a balloon to achieve as near to a round shape as you can. Prepare a paste of flour and water in a bowl; the mixture should have the consistency of thick batter. Rip up the newspaper into strips, dip them in the paste, and cover the balloon in three to four layers of papier-mâché. Leave in a warm place to dry, preferably overnight.

2 Once it is fully dry, pop the balloon with a pin and gently sand the ball shape with fine-grit sandpaper. Paint it with a base coat of white latex paint and then with a plain poster color of your choice.

3 Spatter-paint the ball shape with a variety of colors. Hold the brush of watery paint about 1 inch away from the ball, bend back the bristles with your fingertip, then let them spring back, so that paint spatters onto the shape. Place newspaper underneath where you are working as it can get very messy.

4 Make a hoop to place around the papier-mâché ball. To do this, use a pair of compasses to draw two circles, one inside the other and 1½ inches apart, on colored cardboard. Make sure that you make the diameter of the inner circle large enough to accommodate the size of the ball.

5 Cut out the hoop and decorate it using felt-tip pens or poster paints. Then glue the hoop around the papier-mâché ball.

6 Use pliers to cut a paper clip in half to make a hook. Using a pin, make two holes in the ball ¼ inch apart. Place a blob of glue on each end of the hook and insert it into the ball. Allow to dry.

7 Glue a piece of white mat board about 8 × 8 inches to a piece of gold foil on both sides of the board. Draw about five free-style stars on the now-gold board. Do not worry if they are not perfect.

8 Now cut out the star shapes using either sharp scissors or a craft knife on a cutting mat. Use gold poster paint and a paint brush to touch up the white edges of the stars.

9 Draw a zigzag shape about 1 foot long to represent the Milky Way on black mat board and a moon crescent shape on white board. The moon can be any size you like. Cut out both.

10 Paint the moon yellow and the ping-pong ball pink.

11 Spatter-paint these three shapes with a variety of colors, in the same way as you did the papier-mâché ball. Allow to dry.

12 Cut a paper clip with the pliers as you did in step 7 and glue a hook into the ping-pong ball in the same way. Attach silver thread to the hook in the papier-mâché ball planet and one star. Using a needle and silver thread, join two of the stars together. Hang one star from the crescent moon and hang the ping-pong ball from another star. Keep the threads fairly long at this stage because you may want to make some adjustments when you finally hang them.

13 Using a needle, attach a piece of silver thread to the middle of the zigzag shape at the top. Then, still using the silver-threaded needle, attach each of the objects to the lowest points of the zigzag. You may want to experiment at this stage with the arrangement of the stars and planets.

DOWN ON THE FARM

Most babies are fascinated by mobiles. This one, made using simple, hand-stitched felt animal shapes, would be ideal in a new baby's room, where it will provide hours of pleasure.

YOU WILL NEED

- Tracing paper
- Pencil
- 8 x 10 inch piece of paper
- Scissors
- Pieces of felt (about 6 inches square) in each of the following colors: pink, white, black, blue, turquoise, orange, yellow, brown
- Colored embroidery floss
- Pins and needle
- White craft glue
- 3 wooden skewers

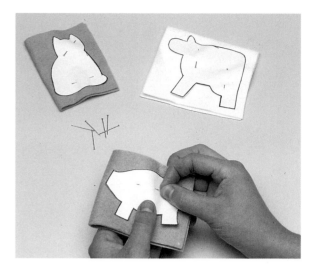

1 Trace the templates of the animals from this book, transfer them to a sheet of paper, and cut them out.

2 Pin each animal template to a double thickness of felt in the appropriate color: pink for the pig, yellow for the cat, blue for the goose, and white for the sheep and cow.

TEMPLATES FULL SIZE

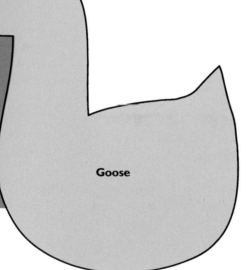

Goose

Pig

Sheep

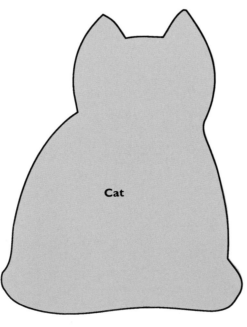

Cat

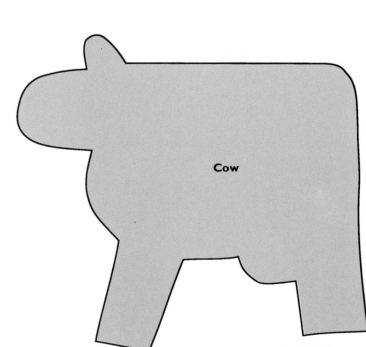

Cow

3 Cut out the felt animal shapes using scissors. Keep the scraps to use as stuffing later.

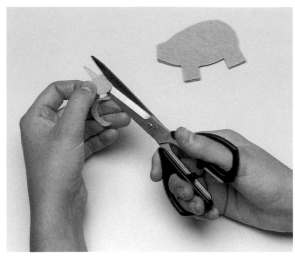

4 Cut out a small spiral for the pig's tail from the leftover pink felt.

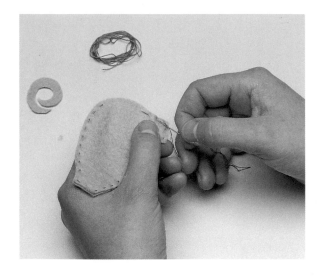

5 Using a strand of embroidery floss in a color that contrasts with that of the animal, handsew the two sides of each animal together around the edge, leaving a gap of about ½ inch to allow for stuffing and, in the case of the pig, for inserting the tail. Leave the needle and thread attached to the animal while you go on to step 6.

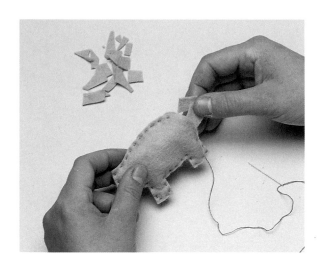

6 Cut the leftover scraps of felt into small pieces and use them to stuff the felt animals. Once the animals are lightly padded, sew up the gap. Remember to add the tail when you make the pig.

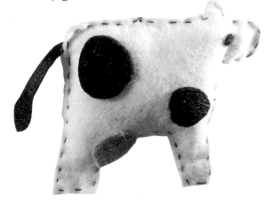

7 From the brown felt, cut out small shapes to make the body marking for the pig. Glue the brown "spots" to both sides of the pig's body. Cut out and attach the details of the other animals in the same way, using appropriate colors: make the cow's udder and spots, the goose's wings, the cat's spots, and the sheep's head and legs. Look at the final picture to see where these go.

8 Using a needle, attach a generous length of embroidery floss to the top of each animal, at a point that will allow the animal to hang level.

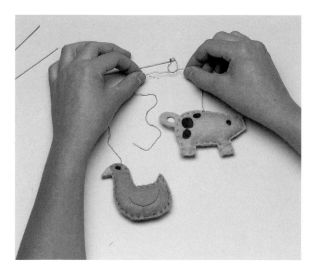

9 Using scissors, shorten the wooden skewers so that two of them measure 4½ inches and the other one measures 9 inches; these will form the struts. Tie the pig and duck at different lengths to the ends of one of the short struts and tie the sheep and cat to the other one in the same way.

10 Attach a length of thread to the middle of each of the short struts. Now attach the two short struts to each end of the long strut, at different lengths. Tie the cow to the middle of the long strut. Tie a piece of thread to the middle of the long strut to suspend it from the ceiling. You may need to move the knotted threads up or down the struts until all the struts and animals are balanced.

SWEET IDEA

• • • • • • • • • • • • • •

This edible sweet mobile would go down a treat at a children's party. Suitable bright-colored candy is threaded on using a needle, and attached to a sturdy painted wooden frame which is decorated with colored beads.

● YOU WILL NEED

- ● 2 feet length of ¼-inch square wooden dowel
- ● Hacksaw
- ● Sandpaper
- ● White craft glue
- ● Poster paint
- ● Mixing palette
- ● Paint brush
- ● Pliers
- ● 9 small screw-in hooks
- ● Scissors
- ● Bright-colored sewing thread
- ● Needle
- ● Assortment of colorful soft candy such as those pictured
- ● 12 wooden beads in assorted colors

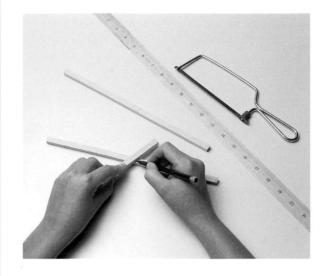

1 Cut two lengths of square dowel 11 inches long using a hacksaw. Mark the center of each length with a groove the width of the dowel itself, and make the groove at a slight slant. Use a spare piece of dowel as a guide to achieve the correct width of groove.

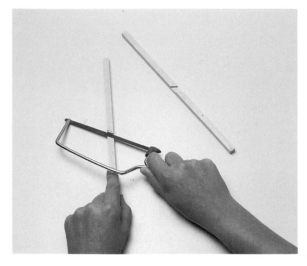

2 Use the hacksaw to cut out the marked groove in both pieces to a depth of about ⅛ inch. The easiest way to cut the groove is to make a number of cuts next to each other, to the correct depth, until the pieces of wood simply crumble away. Smooth away any roughness in the groove with sandpaper.

3 Put a drop of glue into one of the grooves.

4 Place the two pieces of wood together so that the grooves slot into one another.

5 Wait about 30 minutes for the glue to dry, then paint the wooden frame with paint in the poster color of your choice.

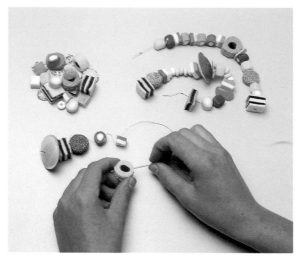

6 When the paint has dried, screw one of the hooks into the top of the frame at the point where the two pieces of wood join: the mobile will hang by this. Screw four hooks into the underside of each wooden bar – keep the spaces between them roughly equal.

7 Cut eight lengths of thread, knot one end and, using a needle threaded at the other end, string the candy. The threads should be 7–10 inches long and should all be about the same length. Try to attach the same weight of candy to each thread so that the mobile hangs evenly.

8 Tie the strings of candy to the hooks, placing strings of equal weight opposite each other. You may need to remove pieces of candy here and there if the mobile is not quite balanced.

9 Glue the wooden beads at regular intervals along the top of the wooden frame. When the glue has dried, use a triple thickness of thread to suspend the mobile (as it is quite heavy) from the central hook on top.

NATURE'S BOUNTY

Gather together a potpourri of dried forms from nature, such as giant seed pods, leaves, and twigs. Attach them with raffia to create this organic, three-dimensional collage.

1 This mobile can depend very much on what you can find outdoors, and it can include all sorts of leaves, twigs, and dried flowers. Here is a selection of materials, some bought, others taken from the backyard. To complete the natural effect, use raffia and twigs.

2 Use thin lengths of raffia; you may need to split it, as it tends to be a little too wide. Tie the things you have collected to the twigs. You may need to use a needle to guide the raffia through some objects. In this mobile, three twigs were decorated to hang from the main twig.

3 When you use the needle to thread through a delicate object, you will need to tie a knot to secure it.

4 Once each of the twigs is fully decorated with bits and pieces, trim away any odd bits of raffia. In our example we have weighted down one side of the mobile slightly by hanging the smallest stick from one of the other small sticks.

5 The top twig – from which all the other twigs will hang – should be decorated. We have attached a row of similar dried flowerheads. Tie one thick piece of raffia to the middle of the main twig and then make a loop at the end from which to suspend it.

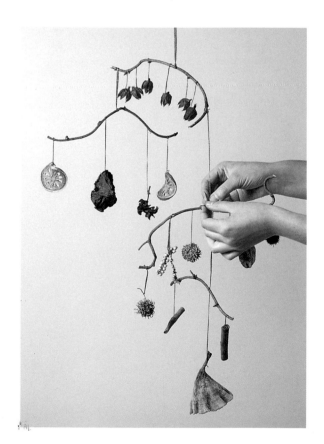

6 Now attach the other decorated twigs and balance the mobile as you add these final details.

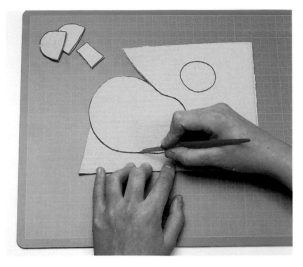

THE BIG BREAKFAST

Cook up this mouthwatering big breakfast mobile using papier-mâché and cardboard. The glossy finish is achieved by applying a coat of clear polyurethane varnish.

● YOU WILL NEED

- Tracing paper
- Pencil
- 11 x 16 inch piece of corrugated cardboard
- Scissors
- White craft glue
- Flour and water
- Bowl
- Newspaper
- Fine-grit sandpaper
- White latex paint
- Mixing palette
- Paint brushes in several sizes
- Poster paints
- Clear gloss polyurethane varnish
- Paper clips
- Long-nosed pliers
- Needle
- About 1 yard galvanized wire, ¹/₂₅ inch in diameter
- Colored sewing thread

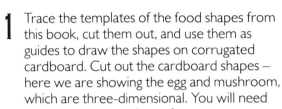

1 Trace the templates of the food shapes from this book, cut them out, and use them as guides to draw the shapes on corrugated cardboard. Cut out the cardboard shapes – here we are showing the egg and mushroom, which are three-dimensional. You will need two sausages, two slices of toast, two tomatoes, four mushroom tops, and two mushroom stalks.

2 Some of the food shapes require extra details – for example, the yolk of the egg – which are also made of cardboard. Glue these on. Glue two mushroom top pieces to the sides of each stalk.

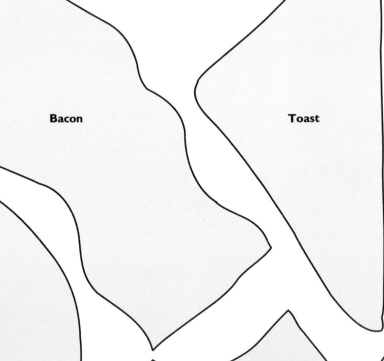

Bacon

Toast

Sausage

Egg white

Egg yolk

Mushroom stalk

Mushroom top

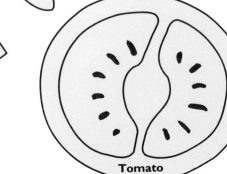

Tomato

3 Mix a flour and water paste in a bowl; it should have the consistency of thick batter. Tear up strips of newspaper, dip them in the paste, and use them to cover the cardboard food shapes – two or three layers should do. Leave in a warm place to dry.

4 Once the papier-mâché shapes have dried, smooth the surface and edges with fine-grit sandpaper. Paint with a base coat of white latex paint.

5 When the base coat has dried, paint the shapes in the appropriate poster-paint colors (yellow for the egg yolk, etc.) and paint in details such as seeds on the tomato slices.

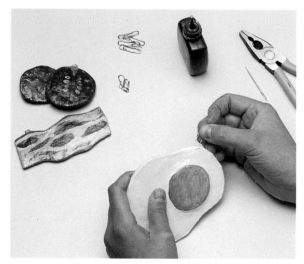

6 Once the shapes are all dry, apply a coat of clear gloss varnish to both sides.

7 Cut three paper clips in half, using pliers, to make hooks. Use a needle to pierce two holes in the edge of each food shape ¼ inch apart. Place a dab of glue on each end of the hooks and insert them into the shapes. Allow to dry.

8 From the wire cut three struts measuring 6 inches and one measuring 11 inches. Use pliers to make a hook at each end of each strut.

9 Paint these struts in colors that go with those of the food shapes – yellow and red.

10 Using different lengths of thread, attach a piece of "food" to each end of each short strut.

11 Tie a piece of thread to the middle of each short strut. You may need to make slight adjustments to find the center of balance. Then attach the three short struts to the long strut, one at each end and one in the middle. To achieve a visually satisfactory mobile, you may need to adjust the lengths of the threads from which the food hangs.

NOAH'S ARK

• • • • • • • • •

"The animals went in two by two" is an endlessly popular theme. This Noah's Ark mobile is a project requiring some skill and is suitable for the more ambitious. A central three-dimensional ark is surrounded by pairs of animals made of colored posterboard with details added in poster paint.

● YOU WILL NEED

- Tracing paper
- Pencil
- 11 x 16 inch pieces of posterboard in each of the following colors: brown, white, yellow, pink, gray
- Scissors
- White craft glue
- Masking tape
- Ruler
- Poster paints
- Mixing palette
- Paint brushes in several sizes
- 1 yard of galvanized wire, $1/16$ inch in diameter
- Silver spray paint
- 2 yards of galvanized wire, $1/25$ inch in diameter
- Long-nosed pliers
- Needle
- Sewing thread
- Paper clip

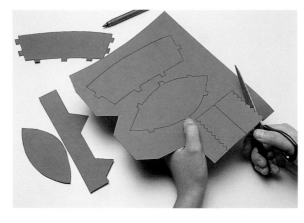

1 Trace the templates from this book for all the ark shapes, enlarge them to full size, transfer them to the brown posterboard and cut them out.

2 Attach one side of the ark to the base by gluing the tabs and then securing them with masking tape. Do the same for the other side and then trim the base if you need to.

TEMPLATES HALF SIZE

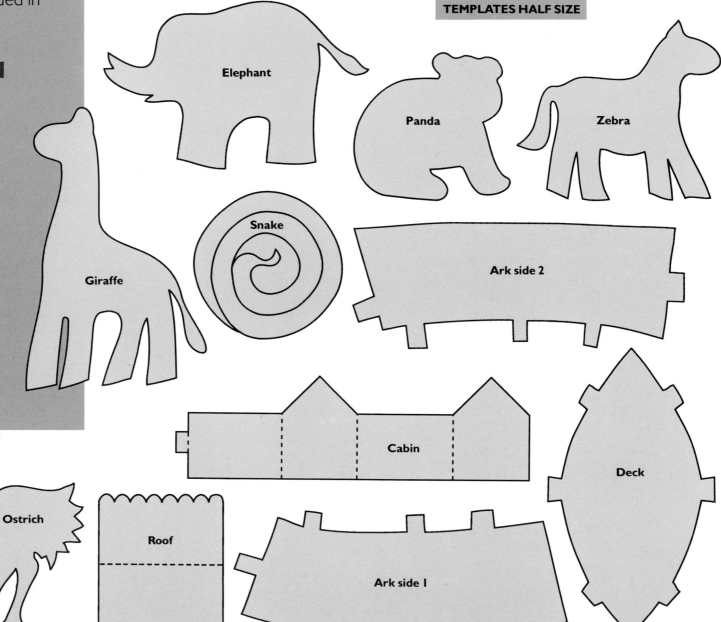

Elephant

Panda

Zebra

Giraffe

Snake

Ark side 2

Ark base

Ostrich

Roof

Cabin

Deck

Ark side 1

3 Once the sides are securely stuck, glue the tabs of the deck and insert it between the two sides of the ark.

4 Using scissors and a ruler, score along the fold lines of the ark pieces – the fold lines are marked on the templates.

5 Fold the cabin and roof pieces along the scored lines. Fold the sides of the cabin around until they meet, then secure by gluing the tab. Now fold the roof along the middle and glue it to the cabin. Glue the cabin to the deck of the ark.

6 Using poster paint, add details such as portholes, roof tiles, deck boards, and so on on the ark.

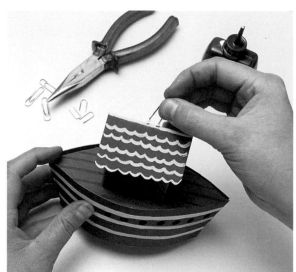

7 Snip a paper clip in half, using the pliers, to create a hook. Use a needle to make two holes in the top of the ark ¼ inch apart. Put a dab of glue on each end of the hook and insert the ends into the holes in the top of the ark. Allow to dry.

8 The completed ark, with all its final details.

9 Trace the templates of the animals from this book, enlarge them to full size, and transfer to posterboard. Cut out two of each shape, using yellow for the giraffes, gray for the elephants, black for the zebras, and so on.

10 Paint both sides of the animals with the appropriate markings: give the zebras stripes, the giraffes patches, and so on.

11 To make the frame, bend a piece of the thicker wire into a circle about 13 inches in diameter. Bind the ends together with a piece of masking tape and spray the tape silver to match the wire.

12 Cut three pieces of thinner wire 14½ inches long to reach across the diameter of the circle like spokes on a wheel. Use long-nosed pliers to twist them around the edge of the main wire circle.

13 Using a needle, attach a length of sewing thread to each animal at a point where it will balance when hung.

14 Use the pliers to cut six lengths of thinner wire about 4 inches long and bend each end of each one into a hook. These will form the struts. Tie a pair of animals to each strut, one at each end.

15 Tie a length of sewing thread to the hook in the top of the ark, then tie the other end firmly to the wires where they cross at the center of the circle. This holds the wires firmly together as well as attaching the ark.

16 To hang up the wheel, cut six threads of equal length and tie them to the sides of the circle where the thinner cross-wires join it. Join all the untied ends of thread together, and once the circular frame is level, tie them in a knot. Create a loop to hang the mobile from.

17 Attach a length of thread to each strut from which the pairs of animals are hanging and tie each strut to the circle where the cross-wires meet the edge of it.

SPARKLING FISH

Create this school of delicately sparkling fish using layers of colored tissue paper and wire. Glistening beads and sequins are included in this project to evoke images of the sea.

● YOU WILL NEED

- 10 feet of galvanized wire, ⅟₂₅ inch in diameter
- Long-nosed pliers
- Masking tape
- Colored tissue paper in a variety of colors
- White craft glue
- Medium paint brush
- Sequins
- Assortment of sparkling beads
- Needle
- Scissors
- Colored cotton thread, the color depending on the color you choose to make your fish

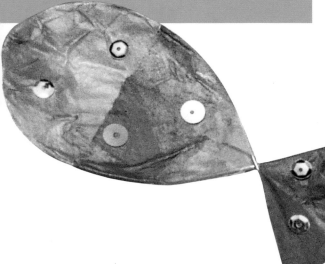

1 Using pliers, cut nine varying lengths of wire – between 7 and 12 inches – depending on how big you want your fish to be. Bend the wire into simple fish shapes as shown and join the ends with a piece of masking tape. The shapes do not have to be perfectly even.

2 Tear colored tissue paper into strips. Use whatever color you like – we chose blues and purples for some fish, and orange and yellow for others. Dilute some white glue with water and coat the tissue-paper strips with this solution using a paint brush.

3 Fold the tissue-paper strips over each wire frame and over each other to cover the entire frame, making sure that they are stuck securely.

4 Add successive layers of tissue paper in a variety of colors – three to four layers should be enough. Avoid soaking the paper because this can cause it to become too soggy and tear. Leave somewhere warm to dry for about 20 minutes. As the solution dries, the tissue will shrink slightly and become quite strong and taut.

5 Now add about five sequins to each side of each fish, using a spot of glue to attach each one. You may prefer to decorate the fish in another way.

6 Gather together some beads of different sizes and colors. Thread a needle with a length of knotted thread in a color that goes with the fish. Thread the needle through the top edge of each fish twice for security.

7 Thread a number of beads onto each thread. Taking the needle through a bead twice will suspend it part of the way up the thread.

8 Using pliers, cut three pieces of thin wire approximately 6 inches long and bend both ends of each one into a hook to hold the threads.

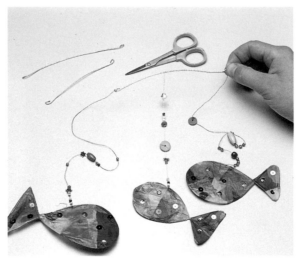

9 Attach three fish to each of the wire struts. Place one at each end and one in the middle, all at different lengths. Tie each thread with a double knot and trim off the loose ends.

10 Tie a length of thread to each of the three struts. Make these quite long so that you can adjust the length when you are hanging the mobile.

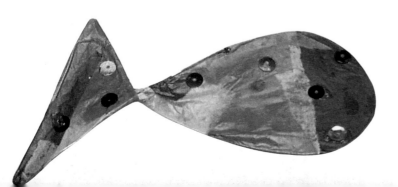

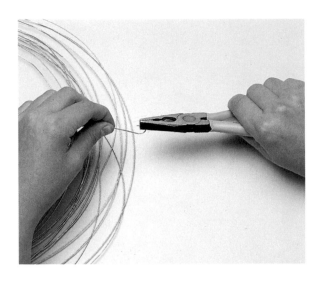

11 Use the pliers to cut a piece of wire about 14 inches long and bend each end into loops as in step 8. This will form the main strut.

12 Attach the three short struts holding the fish to the main strut at varying lengths. placing one at each end and one in the middle. Use a length of thread attached to the middle of the main strut to suspend the mobile.

SWIRLING SPIRALS

This project illustrates a great way of combining fluorescent paper of different colors with simple spinning spirals, resulting in a splendid psychodelic mobile.

YOU WILL NEED

- Scissors
- 4 or 5 16 x 22 inch sheets of heavy fluorescent paper of different colors
- White craft glue
- Pair of compasses
- Pencil
- 11 x 16 inch sheet of mat board
- Craft knife and cutting mat
- Needle
- Colored sewing thread

1 Using scissors, cut out six or seven pairs of squares from fluorescent paper in various colors, measuring anything between 4 × 4 inches and 7 × 7 inches. Glue the pairs of squares together, using different colors on each side. Make lots of different sizes of squares.

2 Using a pair of compasses, draw different-sized circles on the squares. You can draw the circles free-style if you wish.

3 Cut out the circles and then cut into the circles to create spirals.

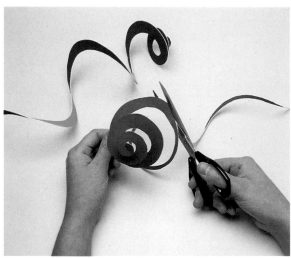

4 Cut into a couple of the spirals to create double spirals.

5 Use a pair of compasses to draw a hoop on mat board with an outer diameter of about 8 inches. The width of the hoop should be about 1 inch. Use a craft knife and cutting mat to cut out the hoop.

6 Glue one side of the hoop to the back of a piece of fluorescent paper and cut away the excess. Repeat with the other side of the hoop so that it is completely covered.

7 Thread a needle with brightly colored sewing thread and knot the end. Pierce the hoop with the needle and attach four separate lengths of thread to the hoop, knotting the end of each one and allowing equal distances between them. Gather up the four lengths of thread together above the hoop and tie in a knot when the hoop hangs level.

8 Thread a needle with the same thread and knot the end. Thread this through the top of a spiral, then attach the spiral to the hoop by piercing the needle through the hoop and knotting it. Repeat for all of the spirals, spacing them evenly and so that they do not restrict each other's movement, and hanging them at different heights. Suspend the mobile and, if necessary, rearrange the spirals until you are happy with the effect.

CHRISTMAS TREE

• • • • • • • • • • • • • • • • • • • •

This year, as an alternative to traditional Christmas decorations, why not construct this easy-to-make decorative Christmas tree? Use corrugated cardboard and add ribbons and stars or anything else you choose to complete this festive mobile.

● YOU WILL NEED

- ● Tracing paper
- ● Pencil
- ● 16 x 20 inch piece of corrugated cardboard
- ● Craft knife and cutting mat
- ● Steel ruler
- ● White craft glue
- ● Green poster paint
- ● Gold spray paint
- ● Silver spray paint
- ● 2 yards of ¼-inch red ribbon
- ● 2 yards of red baby ribbon
- ● Scissors
- ● 16 x 20 inch piece of mat board
- ● 16 x 20 inch pieces of foil paper in several different colors
- ● About 2 yards of gold baby ribbon
- ● Needle
- ● Gold thread
- ● 13 gold beads
- ● Assortment of different sized and colored sequins

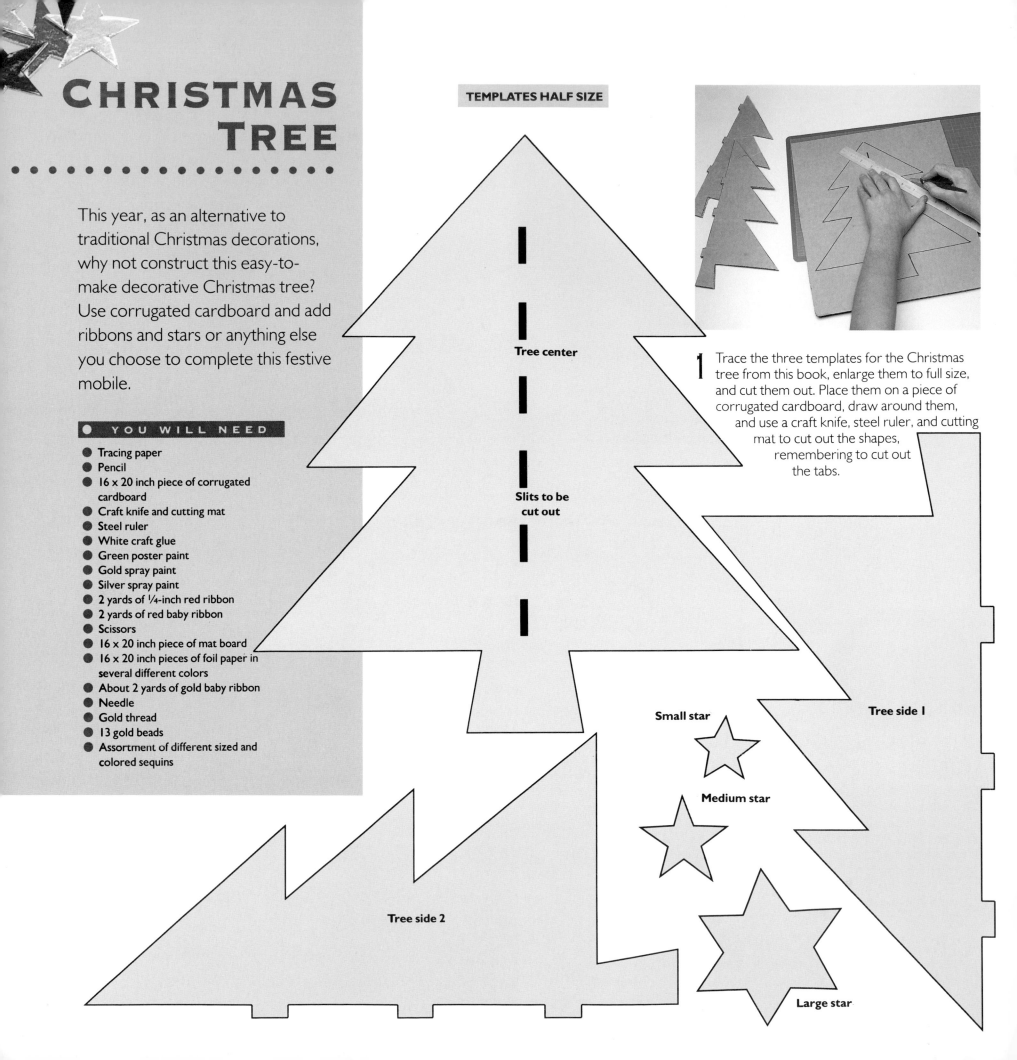

Tree center

Slits to be cut out

1 Trace the three templates for the Christmas tree from this book, enlarge them to full size, and cut them out. Place them on a piece of corrugated cardboard, draw around them, and use a craft knife, steel ruler, and cutting mat to cut out the shapes, remembering to cut out the tabs.

Small star

Medium star

Tree side 1

Tree side 2

Large star

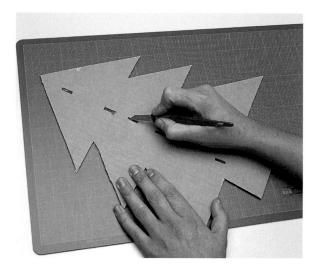

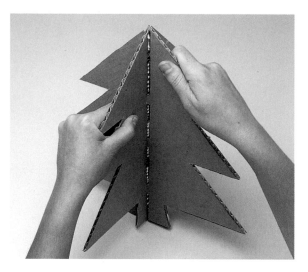

2 Use the craft knife to cut slits in the large tree shape as shown on the template, making sure that they line up with the tabs on the half-tree pieces.

3 Place glue in the slits, on the tabs, and along the straight edge between the tabs. Now fit the three tree pieces together firmly. Leave to dry.

4 Paint the whole tree with green poster paint. When this has dried, spray the tree lightly with gold and then with silver spray paint.

5 Glue a length of ¼-inch red ribbon down each intersection at the middle of the tree. Glue strips of red baby ribbon on each downward slope of the tree and the trunk.

6 Trace the star templates from this book, enlarge them to full size, and transfer the shapes to mat board. Cut four small stars, eight medium stars, and one large one for the top of the tree.

7 Glue one side of each star to the back of foil paper – use several colors. Cut around the star, then glue and cut around the other side in the same way.

8 Use gold baby ribbon to make twelve little bows, one for each "branch" of the tree. Glue a bow to each branch. Thread a needle with gold thread, insert it through one point of a star, then thread on a gold bead. Take the needle up through the tip of a branch and through the middle of the bow, then secure it with a double knot. Repeat for all branches of the tree. Use the small stars for the top four branches.

11 Once the glue is dry, pierce a hole in the top of the star and attach a double length of gold thread by which to suspend the mobile.

12 Glue a bow of gold baby ribbon to the base of the large star on two sides and glue a gold bead above the knot.

9 Use glue to attach assorted sequins to the flat sides of the tree.

10 Insert a dab of glue into the top of the tree and wedge the large star into the top.

JUGGLING CLOWN

The paper fasteners attached to the limbs of this jolly juggling clown allow him to be adjusted into a variety of positions. This, combined with brightly painted ping-pong balls suspended in mid-air, creates a lively and comical mobile.

● YOU WILL NEED

- ● Tracing paper
  Pencil
- ● Scissors
- ● 11 x 16 inch piece of white mat board
  Craft knife and cutting mat (optional)
- ● Poster paints
- ● Mixing palette
  Paint brushes in several sizes
- ○ 11 x 16 inch piece of thin white cardboard
  Long needle
  4 paper fasteners
- ● 3 ping-pong balls
  Colored sewing thread

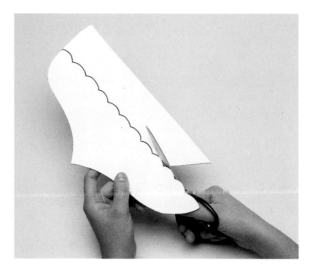

1 Trace the circus-tent template from this book, enlarge it to full size, cut it out, and use it as a guide to draw the shape on white mat board. Cut this out using sharp scissors or a craft knife.

2 Draw stripes on the tent shape with a pencil, then paint them in the poster-paint colors of your choice. Paint both sides of the tent in this way.

3 Trace the clown templates from this book, enlarge them to full size, cut them out, and use them as a guide to draw the shapes on thin white cardboard. Cut these out. You will need two legs and arms!

4 Decorate the clown body pieces as you wish using poster paints. Paint both sides of the clown.

TEMPLATES HALF SIZE

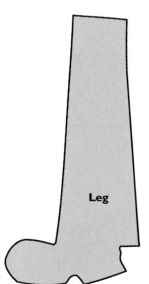

Leg

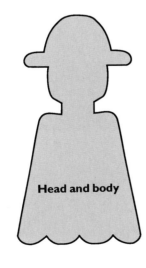

Head and body

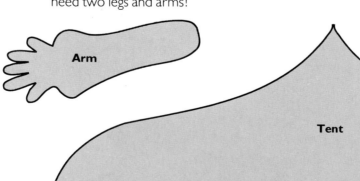

Arm

Tent

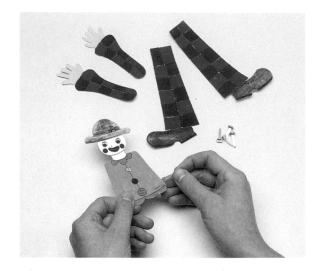

5 Using a long needle or other sharp instrument, pierce small holes in the tops of the clown's limbs, the shoulders, and the points at which the legs will be attached to the body.

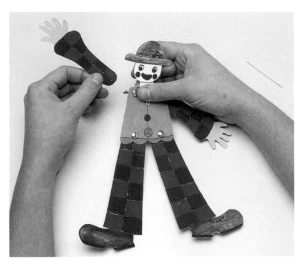

6 Attach the limbs to the body securely with the paper fasteners.

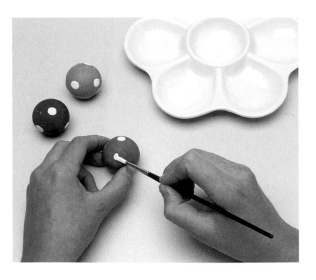

7 Paint three ping-pong balls in bright colors. Add polka dots with white paint.

8 To attach the two outer balls to the tent, simply pass a long needle, threaded with a knotted thread, in and then out of each ball. The knot must be large enough to stop the ball from slipping from the thread. Take the needle through the bottom of the tent and secure it by tying a double knot. Suspend the balls at different lengths.

9 To suspend the middle ball and clown from the tent, first pass the needle, again threaded with a knotted thread, through the top of the clown's head. Make a large knot in the thread about 1½ inches above the clown's head.

10 Now pass the needle through the ping-pong ball – the large knot will keep the ball suspended in "mid-air." Take the needle up through the bottom edge of the tent and secure with a double knot. Try to arrange the balls at different heights.

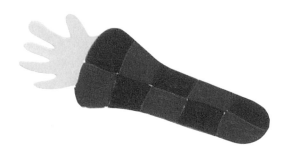

11 Attach a length of thread to the middle of the top of the tent, using a needle to guide it through. The mobile will be suspended from this.

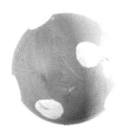

THREE-D DESIGN

Combine the technique of constructing geometric shapes from colored cardboard with simple colorful patterning to create this attractive mobile.

● YOU WILL NEED

- ● Tracing paper
- ● Pencil
- ● 6 pieces of 8 x 10 inch cardboard of different colors
- ● Scissors
- ● Steel ruler
- ● White craft glue
- ● Masking tape
- ● Poster paints
- ● Mixing palette
- ● Small to medium paint brush
- ● About 1 yard of galvanized wire, 1/25 inch in diameter
- ● Long-nosed pliers
- ● Paper clips
- ● Colored sewing thread in a color that matches the shapes

Cone

Cone

Triangular prism

Pyramid

Shallow box

Drum

Cube

Drum

TEMPLATES HALF SIZE

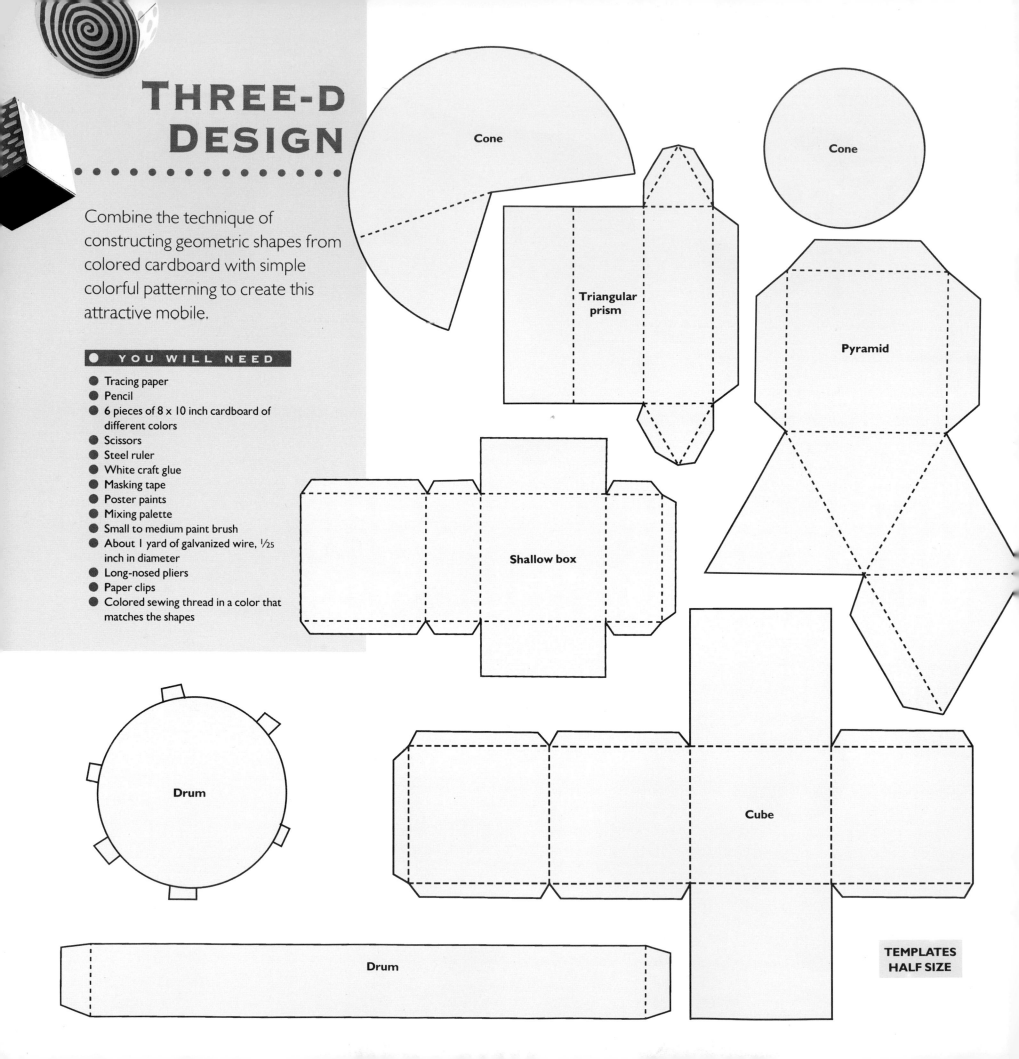

1 Trace the templates for the six geometric shapes from this book, enlarge them to full size, and cut them out. Use them as guides to transfer the shapes to different colored pieces of cardboard, making sure that you draw the fold lines shown on the templates. Cut out the shapes.

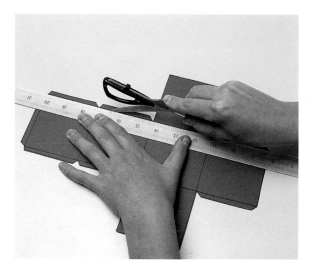

2 Using scissors and a steel ruler, score along the fold lines marked on the shapes.

3 Fold the card along the fold lines.

4 Place glue where necessary and join the shapes firmly together using the tabs. Use masking tape to hold the edges together while the glue dries.

5 When the glue is fully dry, decorate the shapes as you wish using poster paints.

6 Cut three pieces of wire about 5 inches long and one piece about 12 inches long. Using the pliers, bend the ends of the wires into hooks. These will form the struts.

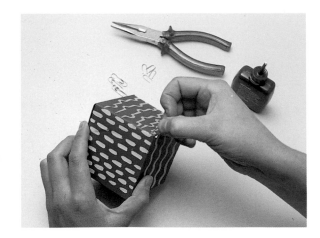

7 Paint the struts in bright poster-paint colors to match the shapes.

8 Using the pliers, cut three paper clips in half to make hanging hooks. Use a needle or pin to make two holes ¼ inch apart at the point on each shape from which you have decided to hang it. Place a dab of glue at both ends of each hook and insert them into the holes you have just made. Allow to dry.

9 Attach two shapes by their hooks to each short strut at different lengths, using colored thread. Make double knots in the thread. Trim off any loose ends.

10 Attach a length of thread to the middle of each short strut at the center of balance. You will find this by easing the tied thread up or down the strut until it hangs level. Now attach the three short struts to the main long strut, hanging one at each end and one in the middle, and all at different lengths so that they do not bump into each other. Also attach a length of thread to the middle of the long strut from which to suspend the mobile. Secure it with a double knot, and once again ease the thread along the strut until you find the center of balance.

BOBBING BOATS

Watch this pretty fleet of gingham sailboats gently sway when wafted by the slightest breeze. The project incorporates fabric, cardboard, and a small amount of painting, resulting in a refreshingly simple mobile.

● YOU WILL NEED

● Tracing paper
● Pencil
● Scissors
● 8 x 10 inch piece of thin red cardboard
● 8 x 10 inch piece of thin blue cardboard
● 4 wooden skewers
● White craft glue
● Small pieces of gingham or other checked fabric in red, white, and blue, about 1 yard altogether
● 8 x 10 inch piece of mat board
● Rickrack in 4 colors, ½ yard of each
● Poster paints
● Mixing palette
● Small paint brush
● Needle
● Colored sewing thread in red, white, or blue

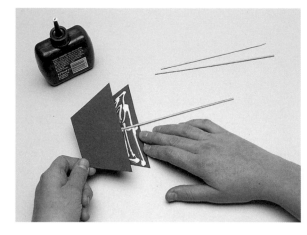

1 Trace the boat hull template from this book and cut it out. Using the template as a guide, cut four hull shapes from the red cardboard and four from the blue.

2 Cut off the sharp ends of four wooden skewers with scissors. Glue a stick to four of the boat hulls (two of each color) to form a mast. Then glue the matching side of each hull in position.

3 To make each sail, glue a piece of gingham fabric to both sides of a square of mat board measuring 5 × 5 inches. You can use a different fabric on each side if you wish.

TEMPLATES FULL SIZE

Sail

Hull

4 Trace the sail template from this book, cut it out, and use it as a guide to draw four sail shapes on the fabric-covered cardboard. Cut these out.

5 Place a line of glue down the middle of each sail (where the mast will go) on one side. Attach a sail to the mast of each boat.

6 Glue a length of rickrack to both sides of each sail.

7 Use poster paints to decorate the sides of the boats.

8 Cut out a square of mat board measuring about 5 × 5 inches. Cut two pieces of gingham fabric, one the same size as the cardboard square, the other slightly bigger. Glue the larger fabric square to the cardboard square and turn over the edges.

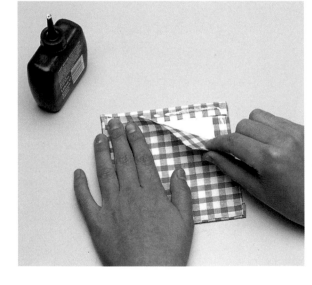

9 Glue the smaller square of fabric to the other side of the carboard to cover the turned edges.

10 Thread a needle with sewing thread and knot the end. Pierce through a corner of the square of fabric-covered cardboard, pull the thread through, then cut it, leaving a length of about 18 inches. Repeat for each corner of the square. Pull the four threads up to meet about 12 inches above the square, and when it lies level, knot the threads together. Using a needle and thread once more, attach a length of thread to the top of each sail. Tie in a knot.

11 Now attach a boat to each corner of the square at different heights, using the needle to take the thread through the cardboard. Secure with a double knot.

FEATHERED FRIENDS

This richly decorated flock of exotic papier-mâché birds combines an interesting "layered" paint technique using sandpaper with bright feathers, sequins, and glitter pens, resulting in a dazzling mobile.

● YOU WILL NEED

- Tracing paper
- Pencil
- Scissors
- 11 x 16 inch piece of corrugated cardboard
- Craft knife and cutting mat
- Flour and water
- Bowl
- Newspaper
- Fine-grit sandpaper
- White latex paint
- Mixing palette
- Paint brushes in several sizes
- Bright poster paints
- Assortment of sequins
- White craft glue
- Glitter pens
- Needle or pin
- Brightly colored feathers
- Long-nosed pliers
- Paper clips
- 1 yard of galvanized wire, 1/16 inch in diameter
- Masking tape
- Silver spray paint
- 1 yard of galvanized wire, 1/25 inch in diameter
- Gold thread

1 Trace the bird template from this book and cut it out. Use it as a guide to draw five bird shapes on corrugated cardboard and cut them out using a craft knife and cutting mat.

2 Mix a flour and water paste in a bowl; it should be the consistency of thick batter. Tear up newspaper into small strips, dip these in the paste and use them to cover the bird shapes with two or three layers of papier-mâché. Leave in a warm place to dry.

3 Once the shapes are completely dry, smooth them using fine-grit sandpaper.

4 Paint the birds with a coat of white latex paint. Allow to dry, then apply an even, thick coat of a bright, strong-colored poster paint — we have used a vibrant pink.

TEMPLATE FULL SIZE

Bird

5 When the paint is dry, apply another coat of white paint. Once this has dried, coat with a further strong color, which will contrast well with the earlier one – we have chosen a bright blue.

6 When the paint is completely dry, gently rub the surface of the bird shapes with sandpaper. You will notice that the first color soon begins to show through the final coat to create a mottled appearance. When you are happy with the effect you have achieved, you can think about adding other details.

7 Paint the beaks yellow, glue on sequins, and decorate with glitter pens and more paint if desired.

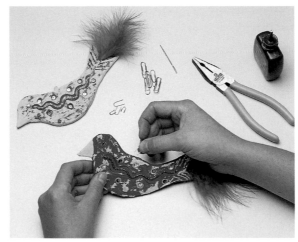

8 Use a needle or pin to make a hole in the tail of each bird at the point of the V and enlarge it if necessary with a piece of wire. Select a feather for each bird, trim it to the required length if it is too long, put a dab of glue on the end, and insert it in the hole.

9 Using pliers, cut three paper clips in half to make hooks to attach to the birds. Make two holes ¼ inch apart in the top edge of each bird, place a dab of glue on both ends of each hook, and insert them into the holes.

10 Using pliers, cut a piece of the thicker wire about 2½ feet long and bend it into a circle with a diameter of about 9 inches. Overlap the edges slightly and use a strip of masking tape to secure the ends, then paint or spray the tape silver.

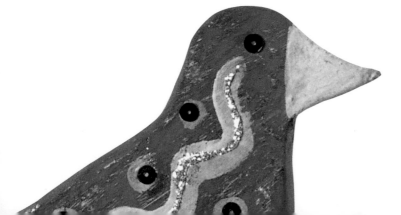

11 Using pliers, cut two pieces of thinner wire about 10 inches long. Attach these across the wire circle, so that they divide it into quarters. Use pliers to wind the ends of the cross-wires around the outer wire circle until they are taut and secure.

12 Cut four lengths of gold thread, each about 2 feet long, and tie each one to the point on the circle where the cross-wires are attached. Gather them together at the top and suspend the circle by them. When it hangs evenly, tie the threads into a knot at the top. Attach a length of gold thread to the hook on each bird. Now attach four of the birds to the wire frame and suspend the fifth bird from the middle of the circle where the wires cross.

UNDERWATER WORLD

Create a magical ocean world of shells and sea creatures. Sparkling beads and silver spray paint are used in this mixed-media project to complete a marine-inspired mobile.

● YOU WILL NEED

- Balloon
- Flour and water
- Bowl
- Newspaper
- Dressmaker's pin
- Fine-grit sandpaper
- White latex paint
- Mixing palette
- Paint brushes in several sizes
- Poster paints
- Silver spray paint
- 11 x 16 inch piece of thin white cardboard
- 11 x 16 inch piece of white mat board
- Tracing paper
- Pencil
- Scissors
- Craft knife
- White craft glue
- About 12 flat beads
- Needle
- Silver thread
- Assortment of sparkling beads
- Long-nosed pliers
- About 1 yard of galvanized wire, 1/16 inch in diameter
- Masking tape
- About 5 1/2 feet of galvanized wire, 1/25 inch in diameter

1 Blow up a balloon, but not fully – just enough to make a round shape. Mix some flour and water into a paste in a bowl; the mixture should resemble thick batter. Tear the newspaper into small strips, dip them into the paste, and use them to cover the balloon with two or three layers of papier-mâché. Leave in a warm place to dry, preferably overnight.

2 When the balloon is dry, pop it with a pin and gently smooth the ball shape with fine-grit sandpaper. Apply a coat of white latex paint. Allow to dry.

3 Apply poster paint to the ball shape – we have chosen purple. Allow to dry.

TEMPLATES FULL SIZE

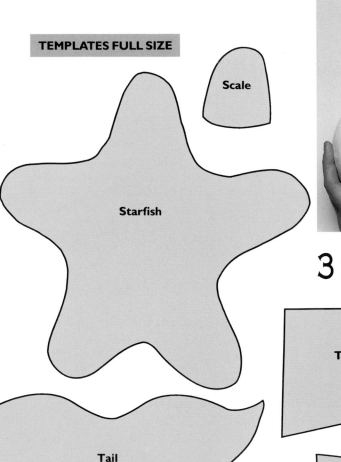

Scale

Starfish

Top fin

Shell

Tail

Bottom fin

Shell

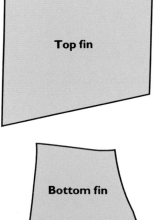

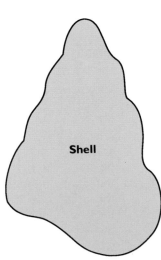

4 Spray the ball with silver spray paint. When this is dry, spatter-paint it with another color. Hold the brush of watery paint about 1 inch away, bend back the bristles with your fingertip, then let them spring back. Lay a piece of thin cardboard and a piece of mat board on newspaper and spray them lightly with the silver spray paint.

5 Trace the templates for the fish's tail and fins from this book and cut them out. Use them as a guide to draw the shapes on the silver-sprayed mat board, then cut these out with scissors. Cut about thirty scales from the silver-sprayed thin cardboard.

6 Use a pencil to mark on the fish the positions of the fins and tail. Cut slits of the appropriate size using a craft knife. Place glue in the slits and insert the fins and tail. Allow to dry.

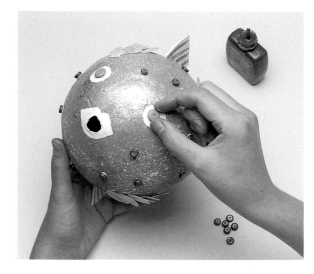

7 Attach the scales in clusters on the body of the fish by applying glue to the narrower end of each one. Bend them slightly before you attach them and make sure that they overlap.

8 Paint stripes on the fins and tail of the fish. Make a small hole for the mouth using a craft knife and paint lips around it. Paint the eyes.

9 Use glue to attach flat beads or any other decoration you may want to add. Glue larger beads onto the eyes, too.

10 Trace the templates for the shells and starfish from this book and cut them out. Use them as a guide to draw and cut out a total of eight shapes.

11 Paint the shapes in a variety of poster-paint colors – we have chosen pastels.

12 Add more detail to the shapes to bring out their shell-like qualities. Spatter-painting is a useful technique at this stage, too.

13 Thread a needle with silver thread and use it to pierce a hole in each shape. Knot the thread to secure it. Now thread some sparkling beads at intervals along each thread: do this by taking the needle through each bead twice.

14 Use pliers to cut a piece of the thicker wire 27 inches long and bend it into a circle with a diameter of about 8 inches. Secure the two ends together using a small strip of masking tape. Spray or paint the masking tape silver to match the wire.

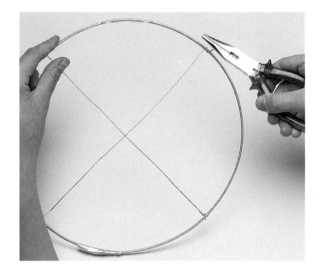

15 Cut two pieces of the thinner wire about 10 inches long. Use pliers to bend the ends of these two pieces of wire around the circle so that they cross over one another, dividing the circle into quarters. The wires should be taut and rigid.

16 Cut four pieces of silver thread about 20 inches long and attach each one to the wire circle at the point where a thinner wire meets it. Pull all the threads up above the wire frame and play around with the balance until the frame is level, then tie the threads together in a knot. Attach the shells and starfish to the frame so that they are equal distances apart. Pierce the top of the round fish's fin with needle threaded with silver thread, add a couple of beads, and tie it to the circular frame at the point where the wires cross in the middle.

HOT-AIR BALLOONS

One of the most basic techniques in papier-mâché involves molding paper around a balloon, and what could be more appropriate than to use this process to create this stunning trio of hot-air balloons?

● YOU WILL NEED

- 3 balloons
- Flour and water
- Bowl
- Newspaper
- Dressmaker's pin
- Fine-grit sandpaper
- Pair of compasses
- Craft knife
- White latex paint
- Mixing palette
- Paint brushes in several sizes
- Pencil
- Poster paints
- Clear gloss polyurethane varnish
- 3 pieces of 8 x 10 inch thin cardboard in different colors
- White craft glue
- Needle
- Colored sewing thread
- Long-nosed pliers
- Paper clips
- 1 wooden skewer

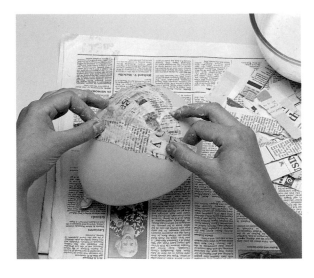

1 Blow up three balloons to slightly different sizes. Mix a paste of flour and water in a bowl; it should be the consistency of thick batter. Rip up newspaper into strips roughly 1 x 4 inches, dip them in the paste, and use them to cover the balloons with three or four layers of papier-mâché. Try to avoid air bubbles and lumps forming as you go. Leave in a warm place to dry, preferably overnight.

2 Once they are fully dry, burst the balloons with a pin, then gently sand the shapes using fine-grit sandpaper. Draw a circle with a diameter of 2–3 inches on the base of each balloon and cut it out with a craft knife. Smooth any rough edges using the sandpaper.

3 Paint the balloons with a coat of white latex paint and allow to dry thoroughly.

4 Using a pencil, lightly draw designs on the balloons. Paint with poster paints.

5 Once the paint is dry, apply a coat of clear gloss varnish.

6 To make a basket, cut out a strip of colored cardboard about 2 x 7 inches. Glue the two ends together, slightly overlapping them, to form a cylinder, and decorate with paint.

7 Place the cylinder on a piece of the same color cardboard, draw around it, cut this out, and glue it to the base of the basket. Repeat this step for the other two baskets, but make them all different colors.

8 Use pliers to cut two paper clips in half, creating four hooks (only three of which you will need). Using a large needle, pierce two holes ¼ inch apart at the top of each balloon. Place a dab of glue on each end of each hook and insert them into the holes.

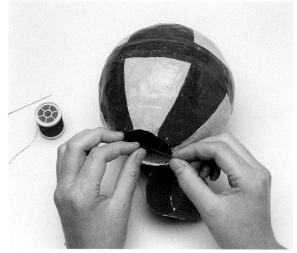

9 Thread a needle with thread in a color that matches the balloons. Make a knot in the end. Pierce the needle through the top edge of one of the baskets. Take the needle through the hole twice to make it secure. Now pierce the needle through the matching balloon's base at the edge of the circle. Allow 2–3 inches of thread between the basket and the balloon, and secure it by taking the needle through the hole once more and knotting it. Repeat this on the other side and on the other two baskets and their balloons.

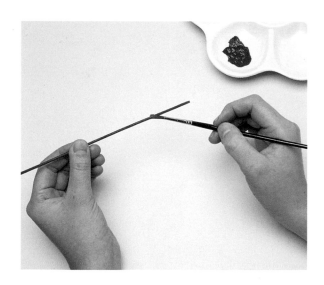

10 Cut off and discard the sharp end of a wooden skewer. Paint the stick a color to match the balloons: this will form the strut from which the mobile will hang.

11 Attach a double-thickness of thread to the middle of the strut to hang the mobile from. Now tie one end of a length of thread to each balloon hook and the other end to the strut, attaching one balloon in the middle and one at each end. Suspend the balloons at different heights.

DIVING DOLPHINS

This mobile beautifully captures the action of glistening dolphins diving through hoops. Colored cardboard, glitter paints, sequins, and metallic sprays are all used to construct and decorate this attractive mobile.

● YOU WILL NEED

- Pair of compasses
- Pencil
- 8 x 10 inch pieces of thin cardboard in several different colors, including blue and gray
- Scissors
- Poster paints
- Mixing palette
- Medium paint brush
- Glitter pens
- White craft glue
- Assorted sequins
- Tracing paper
- Newspaper
- Silver spray paint
- Gold spray paint
- Needle
- Silver thread
- 2 wooden skewers
- 1 foot of galvanized wire, ¹⁄₂₅ inch in diameter
- Long-nosed pliers

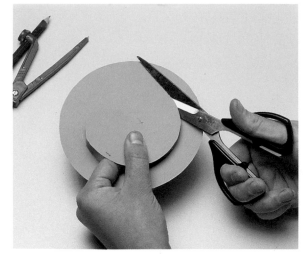

1 Using a pair of compasses, draw five hoops on thin cardboard in different colors (but keep the blue and gray pieces for the dolphins). To make each hoop, draw two circles, one inside the other and 1–1½ inches apart. The diameter of the inner circle should be 4–5 inches.

2 Carefully cut out the hoops with a pair of sharp scissors.

3 Using poster paints, decorate the hoops with designs of your choice. Painting around the outer and inner rims gives good definition. Use glitter pens to add extra richness to the hoops, and glue on some sequins for a finishing touch.

4 Trace the dolphin template from this book and cut it out. Use it as a guide to draw five dolphins on the blue and gray card. Cut these out.

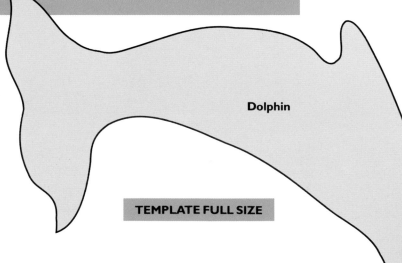

Dolphin

TEMPLATE FULL SIZE

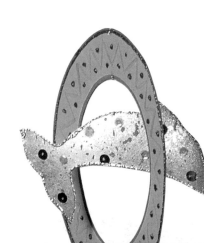

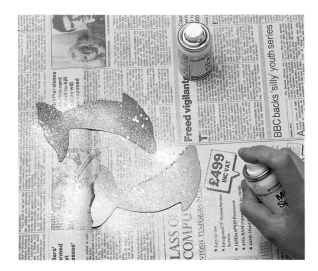

5 Place the dolphins on a sheet of newspaper and spray them lightly on one side with silver, then with gold paint. Repeat this on the other side.

6 Add extra color by spatter-painting one side of the dolphins. Hold the brush of watery paint about 1 inch away, bend back the bristles with your fingertip, then let them spring back. Allow to dry, then repeat this on the other side of the dolphins.

7 As a finishing touch, add sequins to the dolphins with glue and outline each dolphin with a silver glitter pen.

8 Use a needle to attach a length of silver thread – about 5 inches – to each dolphin.

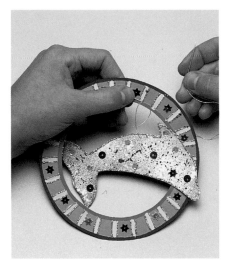

9 Now attach each dolphin to the inside of a hoop, using the needle to guide the thread once more. Pass the needle through twice and finish with a double knot. Trim any loose ends. The dolphin should be suspended in such a way that it does not touch the hoop.

10 Cut off the sharp ends of two wooden skewers with scissors. If you like, paint the sticks with poster paints. These will form the struts.

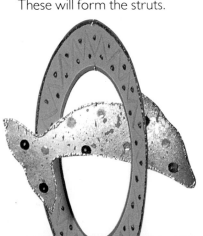

11 Thread a needle with silver thread, longer than before, and pass it through the rim of each hoop near the edge, directly above where the dolphin hangs. Secure the thread with a double knot. Attach a pair of hooped dolphins to each strut, one at each end. Adjust the lengths of the threads so that the dolphins hang at different heights.

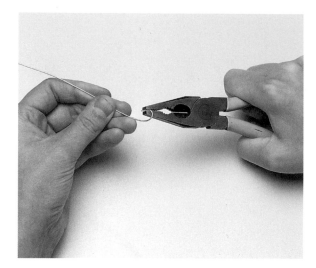

12 Cut a piece of wire about 11 inches long, using pliers to bend the ends into hooks.

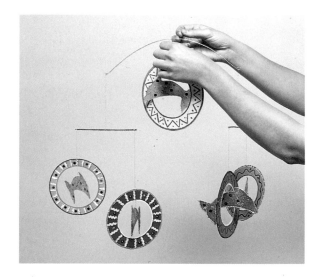

13 Tie a piece of silver thread to the middle of each wooden strut, then suspend the struts from the hooks at each end of the wire. Attach the fifth hooped dolphin to the middle of the wire on a short thread. Secure all the threads with double knots. The mobile hangs from a length of silver thread attached to the middle of the wire.

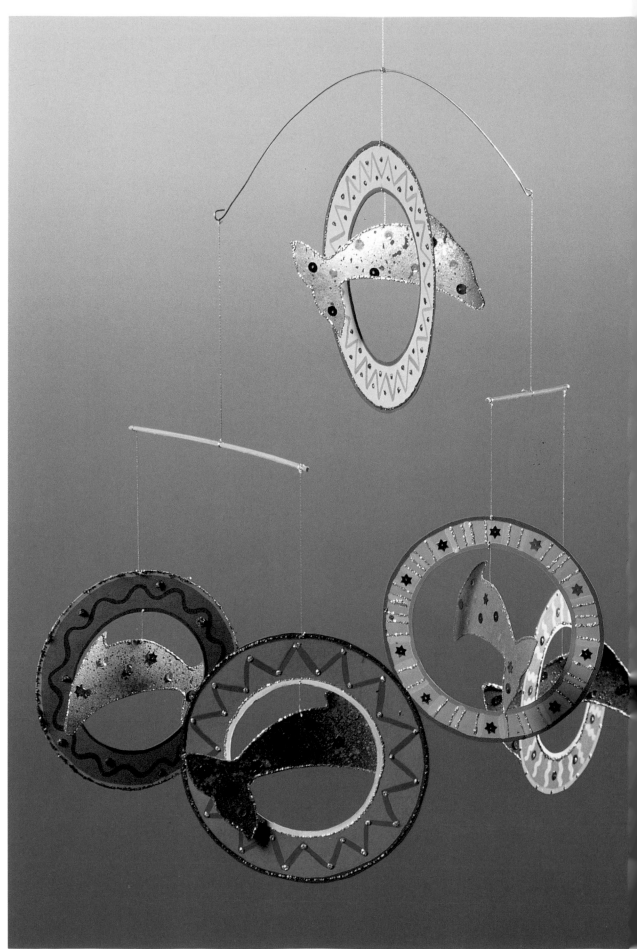